DRUGS AND FITTING IN

Many teens find that they can actually have more fun without using drugs.

THE DRUG ABUSE PREVENTION LIBRARY

DRUGS AND FITTING IN

by George Glass

THE ROSEN PUBLISHING GROUP, INC.

NEW YORK

The people pictured in this book are only models. They in no way practice or endorse the activities illustrated. Captions serve only to explain the subjects of photographs and do not in any way imply a connection between the real-life models and the staged situations.

Published in 1998 by The Rosen Publishing Group, Inc.
29 East 21st Street, New York, NY 10010

Library of Congress Cataloging-in-Publication Data

Glass, George, 1970—
    Drugs and fitting in / by George Glass.—1st ed.
    p. cm. — (The drug abuse prevention library)
    Includes bibliographical references and index.
    Summary: Discusses teen culture in America and how drug use has become part of that culture; offers guidance for teens on how to say no to drugs and still fit in..
        ISBN 0-8239-2554-4
        1. Teenagers—Drug use—United States—Juvenile literature. 2. Drug abuse—United States—Psychological aspects-Juvenile literature. 3. Peer pressure in adolescence—United States—Juvenile Literature. [1. Drug abuse. 2. Peer pressure.]
        I. Title. II. Series.
        HV5824.Y68G5 1998
        362.29'0835'0973—dc21   97-44528
                                                                        CIP
                                                                        AC

Manufactured in the United States of America

Contents

Peer pressure is a big influence on teens when they decide to experiment with drugs.

CHAPTER 1

Drugs, Teen Culture, and Style

"*This is so stupid," thought Jeff. "I never believed I would actually have to deal with peer pressure." Jeff had always laughed at antidrug TV shows and movies, where teens in leather jackets would taunt the wholesome, all-American kids for not taking drugs. "You're not cool, like us," they always said.*

But that's not how it happened to Jeff. The people telling him to try drugs were his friends. They were angry with him because he wouldn't take drugs with them. They laughed at him and told him how the drug would open his mind if he tried it. But he didn't want to try it. "I just think it's a bad idea, and I have my own reasons for choosing not to take drugs," he said. Why couldn't they just deal with it? They seemed to think that

8 *he had to take drugs to be a part of what was happening around him.*

What exactly is "teen culture"? And how did it become linked to drug use? Teen culture is a term sometimes used to describe the lifestyle of teens. It includes young people's favorite fashions, music, movies, books, magazines, and many other types of art and entertainment. It also includes pastimes, attitudes, and states of mind. It is the invisible thread that connects teens all across the country and frequently beyond those borders.

When young people from the east coast to the west coast tune in to MTV at the same time to watch the premiere of the new Coolio video, American teen culture is being shaped. When the same jacket, hat, or haircut starts springing up in high schools in both small towns and big cities, you can actually see teen culture as it develops.

Fitting In

Why is teen culture so important? Most teens are seeking to define themselves outside of their families. For that reason, approval from their peers may mean more than ever. You may find, as many teens

Many teens like to keep current with fashion in clothing, hair-styles, and music. Drugs are sometimes used as another way to fit in.

10 | do, that you want to "belong" to a group. Being part of teen culture can make a person feel that he or she "belongs."

For you, belonging might mean joining the football team, the drama club, or the school band. Or, it may mean identifying with something beyond the school, such as a church or synagogue. Or it may mean identifying with a musician or actor, and wearing clothes similar to those worn by that person.

But for many teens, keeping current with fashion in clothing, hairstyles, music, and sometimes drug use is the way they try to fit in. This is an important time for teens, who are finding out who they are as people with identities separate from their parents. They may be experimenting with ideas or experiences that their parents would not approve of. Sometimes teens are drawn to mainstream culture, and sometimes they are drawn to subcultures.

Teen Subcultures

Mainstream teen culture is what most teens like. But many young people like things that are different from the mainstream. These teens sometimes form teen subcultures, which are groups of young people with similar attitudes and styles that are different from the mainstream. For example, young punks and hippies are examples of two very different subcultures.

Fashion, Drugs, and Teen Subculture: Some Connections

When teen subcultures form, they usually find ways to separate themselves from the mainstream. Often, their fashion choices set them apart from others in the mainstream. Tattoos, body piercing, and brightly colored hair might be the general style of one subculture, while torn jeans, long hair, and bandannas could be the favorite look of another. Subcultures almost always influence mainstream culture. Using drugs is another way in which some teen subcultures define their styles. For example, "rave culture," which developed in England during the 1980s, was based largely on the use of the drug Ecstasy (a hallucinogen). Many young people in that subculture took Ecstasy to gain extra energy and an altered state of mind so they could keep dancing for long periods of time. They also wore clothes that showed popular symbols of Ecstasy, such as yellow "smiley" faces and neon flowers.

12 | *From Subculture to Mainstream*
It is interesting to look at rave as an
example of how a subculture spreads into
the mainstream. When it started out,
rave was considered an "outlaw" subculture. The all-night dance parties, called
"raves," were fueled by large quantities of
drugs such as Ecstasy, LSD, and speed.
Raves were held in large outdoor fields,
and the invitations to them never revealed
the locations. That way, there was less
chance of the police raiding the events for
drugs. People could find out about a rave
only by word-of-mouth, which made it
seem more exciting and exclusive to those
who attended.

But slowly, rave music was picked up
by DJs in mainstream nightclubs and
used by mainstream artists. Popular fashion designers started incorporating rave
styles into their clothing lines. By the
time rave hit the United States in the late
1980s, it did not mean the same thing.
Many American club promoters had "rave
nights," which simply meant that rave
music was played.

But along with the music came the
use of Ecstasy. Ecstasy became a very
common club drug, and many young
people in the mainstream teen culture

Many teens in the rave subculture took Ecstasy to gain extra energy and an altered state of mind.

14 | began taking it frequently. The idea of "clubbing," or going out to clubs, without Ecstasy was unthinkable for many people.

Raves, which had started out as part of a subculture, became a mainstream activity. Rave clothing, which began as the fashion of a subculture, emerged into mainstream fashion.

CHAPTER 2

Some History on Drugs and Teens

*R*ave is not the only drug-related sub-culture to have had a big impact on the mainstream culture. Many fashions and trends have involved young people's use of drugs. Some teen subcultures have even been created around drug use.

Drugs sometimes play a big part in teen culture, but how did they get there? Why haven't they gone out of fashion? And how have young people's attitudes about drugs changed over time?

Drugs, Experimentation, and the 1960s

Those questions lead us back to a very important time in the history of the United States, the 1960s. It was a time of great change, and many people were con-

The 1960s was a time of rebellion against authority and experimentation with illegal drugs.

fused and excited about the things that were taking place.

Many people, including teens, were rebelling against authority. In a way not seen before in the United States, young people and others questioned accepted ideas about politics, religion, values, and just about every other area of life. Many of the changes were positive. People organized and stood up for things that they believed in. Many young people wanted to work toward world peace and to end the United States' involvement in the Vietnam War.

Before the 1960s, many Americans thought that only a few people used drugs. Then suddenly it seemed as if

drugs were being used and talked about | *17*
everywhere, by all kinds of people. It was
part of the new style and culture that
young people were creating for themselves. Like many teens today, they
wanted to live in a world that was
different from the one in which their
parents grew up.

Sometimes the experimentation with
illegal drugs had deadly results. For example, two of the most respected rock artists of the 1960s, Jimi Hendrix and Janis
Joplin, died of drug-related causes. Unfortunately, the trend continues today with
members of popular bands like Smashing
Pumpkins, Hole, and Blind Melon dying
of drug overdoses.

Many parents in the 1960s were confused and frustrated by the way their sons
and daughters looked. The "hippie" look
became popular. Men were letting their
hair grow long, which was shocking at the
time. Women began wearing their skirts
much shorter than ever before. Fashion
reflected the rebelliousness of the time,
and it was in this atmosphere that drugs
became especially fashionable among
teens.

Of course, not everyone who looked
like a hippie used drugs. And not every-

18 | one who used drugs looked like a hippie.

Rebellion on the Dance Floor

Punk rock and disco are good examples of very different fashion subcultures that emerged in the 1970s. Punk rock traveled from Great Britain to the United States, bringing violence in both lyrics and music to American teens. Torn clothing, spiked hair, safety pins as earrings, steel-toed boots, and other fashion elements became popular. Drug use was a part of the rebelliousness of punk. There was no single drug of choice, but heroin is commonly associated with punk and its motto: "No Future." The fashion choices and attitudes of the punks were, in part, a reaction against the peace and love attitudes of the hippies.

Disco also emerged in the 1970s, bringing with it the mirrored balls and bright lights of the nightclub scene. Its glitzy, flashy attitude was reflected in the fashions of the time. Shiny fabrics and tight, glittery clothes became popular. Cocaine was most often the drug associated with this trend, probably to keep up energy levels for all-night dancing.

Both of these trends in the music scene, as well as many others since, have been reflected by changes in mainstream fashion. Many have also often been associated with drug use. For teens who want to be part of the culture of the times, it has always been tempting to step into the drug scene.

Drug Chic

Drugs often seem glamorous to young people. Drugs may represent a way to rebel and to be fashionable.

Why do drugs seem to be the latest fashion? In the 1990s, there has been a major increase in heroin use among musicians and other celebrities. Heroin use was portrayed in popular films such as *Trainspotting* and *Pulp Fiction*. Both films do, however, show the darker side of heroin addiction and overdose.

Drug abuse is often portrayed by the media as part of the rock musician's lifestyle. Unfortunately, drug abuse is common in the music world. This has sometimes led to tragedy. Shannon Noon of the band Blind Melon died of a cocaine overdose in 1995. Kurt Cobain, lead singer of Nirvana, was struggling with a heroin addiction at the time he committed suicide. Smashing Pumpkins' keyboardist Jonathan Melvoin died from

Many teens who are fashionable choose to be drug-free.

an overdose of heroin and alcohol. Yet
in spite of these tragedies, many young
people still take drugs to imitate their
music idols. Even Kurt Cobain talked
about how Rolling Stones' guitarist Keith
Richards made heroin seem glamorous.

Drug chic is also found in the world of
fashion. In recent years, some popular
models have been styled to resemble
heroin addicts, with sunken cheeks, dark
circles around their eyes, bony bodies,
and pasty skin. This trend has also been
called "junkie chic" because it suggests a
connection between drug addiction and
glamour.

Anyone who has actually been addicted to drugs can tell you that drug
addiction is far from glamorous. Drugs
can do major damage to users' bodies
and can even lead to death. Drug addicts
often destroy relationships with the
people who are most important to them.
Rather than making you look like the
glamorous celebrity you admire, drugs
can make you look and feel terrible.

Fashion Among Friends
Another element of fashion is what is
popular among your friends or people
you admire. This may reflect mainstream

22 | culture, a subculture, or a mixture of both. Your group of friends may like to wear certain styles of clothing, or to listen to certain kinds of music. Sometimes teens consider drug use a part of the fashion of their group.

Melissa was fifteen. She and her family lived in a small town in Pennsylvania.

Even though she was always considered "the weird girl" at her school, she had a group of friends with whom she felt comfortable. They all liked British pop music by bands like Elastica and Pulp, and they loved to experiment with their hair and clothes. Most of what they wore came from the Salvation Army, and their hair was always either shaved off or bleached white. Everybody else thought that Melissa and her friends were trying to be strange and shocking, but they were really just styling themselves in a way that they liked. When they were together, it didn't seem strange at all.

Another thing they liked to do together was smoke pot. Melissa and her friend Junior did it only occasionally, while other members of the group smoked it every day. But they all smoked pot when they were together. They liked the way it made everything seem funny, and it seemed to bond them together in some way.

They would all talk about trying other

Many young people still take drugs to imitate their music idols.

drugs, but none of them had actually tried anything else. Melissa had never really thought about the fact that she was smoking pot. It just seemed to be what everybody did, and it was no big deal. She had grown up watching people do it in movies and listening to people sing about it in songs. Some of her favorite bands used the marijuana leaf as a symbol on their clothes and CDs.

Melissa's father got a new job that required the family to move to a suburban town in New Jersey. Both of her parents liked the idea of living close to New York City, but Melissa was not pleased about the move.

After moving, it didn't take long for Melissa to find the people she wanted to know. They looked different from the "weird

24 | *kids" at her old school, but they were defi-
nitely the weird kids. They didn't look alike.
Each one had his or her own unique style.*

*At first, Melissa was worried that they
wouldn't like her, but then they came to her
and introduced themselves. Soon she was
hanging out with them every day. She in-
stantly clicked with a girl named Tonisha.
Tonisha was a beautiful African American
girl who wore her hair in a stylish Afro,
usually with a silky blouse and flared jeans.
Melissa liked Tonisha's fierce attitude and
sense of style.*

*One night the two girls were talking in
Melissa's room. Melissa anxiously asked
Tonisha what it was like to live so close to
New York City. "Well, it's not really a big
deal for me, because I'm from Los Angeles,"
Tonisha explained. "We like to go into the
city to the big dance clubs sometimes."
Melissa cautiously brought up the topic of
drugs. She suddenly realized that she hadn't
had a joint since she left Pennsylvania.*

*Tonisha said that she had never taken
drugs and did not intend to start. Melissa
was a little shocked. She had just assumed
that since Tonisha dressed in her own style
and went out to big nightclubs, she must have
done some drugs. "It's not my thing," said
Tonisha. "I just like to dance. I also love*

clothes, and I want to be a fashion designer."
Tonisha explained that she would much ra-
ther save money to go to design school than
waste it on drugs. Also, she knew that a drug
habit and the health problems that come with
it would only get in the way of her goals, and
she was very *ambitious.*

"Some of the other guys take drugs,"
Tonisha said. "I don't get on their cases
about it, but it gets on my nerves when they
pass out in the bathroom or fall on top of me
in line at the club." She invited Melissa to
join them for a night out sometime. Melissa
could hardly wait, although she was more
confused than ever about drugs.

Tonisha was so fabulous, and she was so
sure of herself. Melissa wished that she could
be that. She was glad she no longer used
marijuana like her old friends, but she was
still curious about other drugs.

Don't Be Too Quick to Judge

Some people, including teens, mistakenly
believe that everybody who dresses in
the style of a subculture takes the drugs
associated with that style. But this is not
always true. For example, Moby, one of
rave music's most respected artists, has
spoken out against drugs and the fact that
they have destroyed lives. And many teens

26 | who are fashionable choose to remain drug-free.

It is also a common mistake to believe that teens in the mainstream do not use drugs. Young people from all walks of life use drugs—rich and poor, from all backgrounds, in cities and in suburbs. You cannot always tell just by looking at a person whether or not he or she uses drugs.

Also, because subcultures often influence mainstream culture, many people who may not "look" the part end up doing things—including using drugs—that were formerly done only by members of a subculture.

CHAPTER 3

Disadvantages of Drug Use

*S*ome people believe that all drugs are simply "bad." This is not necessarily true. Many drugs are used to cure diseases and save lives. In fact, some drugs that are now illegal started out as possible treatments for various physical and mental illnesses. Later, these drugs were found to be too dangerous and addictive to be used as medicine for most people.

Using drugs without the guidance of a doctor can be dangerous. Drugs from the street could be cut (mixed) with anything, including any number of deadly substances. Also, many young people who believe they are taking drugs for fun are actually feeding an addiction.

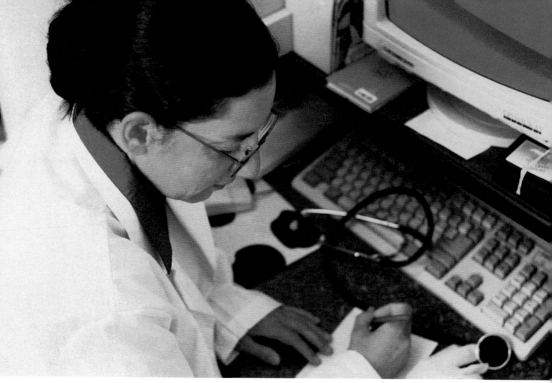
Some illegal drugs were first prescribed as medicines.

Drugs and Their Effects

Hallucinogens
Hallucinogens are drugs such as marijuana, hashish, LSD, peyote, magic mushrooms, mescaline, PCP (angel dust), and Ecstasy. They cause the user to see, hear, and feel differently.

Hallucinogens can lead to depression and possible brain damage. Users of hallucinogens also risk terrifying "bad trips."

Amphetamines
Amphetamines (speed) and methamphetamine (crystal meth, ice, crank) are drugs that speed up the user's mind and body.

They are highly addictive, and withdrawal from them is extremely difficult and painful. Speeding up one's system too much can cause injury to the mind and body and even death.

Depressants

Depressants slow down the user's mind and body. Some of the most popular depressants among young people are narcotics such as heroin and China White (a cheaper and more dangerous form of heroin), alcohol, and the nightclub favorite "Special K." Like amphetamines, these drugs are extremely addictive and difficult to withdraw from. Heroin users can contract HIV (the virus that causes AIDS) by sharing needles with someone who already has HIV when they inject the drug.

Although many young people consider alcohol harmless because it is legal and they have seen adults drink, there are many drawbacks to using alcohol. Drinking can severely damage your liver and kidneys. Drunk driving endangers you and others on the road. And alcohol addiction, or alcoholism, affects people of all ages.

Drug use can cause depression and possible brain damage.

Inhalants

Inhalants are often products that can be found in any household. Young people sometimes sniff glue, gasoline, and typewriter correction fluid for a quick "head rush." These drugs can lead to heart failure and unpleasant side effects such as headaches, dizziness, and sometimes convulsions.

Cocaine and Crack

These drugs are classified as narcotics. People use them because of the brief, intense high and feeling of power they can create in the user. But both are very addictive and can cause severe paranoia and loss of self-control. Each dosage of crack is cheap, which makes it seem like an inexpensive drug habit to maintain. But because it is so addictive, the cost adds up quickly.

The Dangers of Drugs

Tonight was finally the night. Melissa was going to join her new friends for a night out at one of New York City's biggest nightclubs. Tonisha picked Melissa up in her beat-up old car, and they drove into the city together. As they approached the line outside the club,

32 | *Melissa recognized two members of the group, Tommy and Al.*

Tommy seemed especially hyper. He was wearing baggy jeans and a black baseball cap, and his skin looked clammy and pasty. "Well, it's about time," he shrieked. Tonisha whispered to Melissa, "Tommy's coked up again. It makes him irritable."

"I heard that," Tommy snapped. "I am not irritable." Then he sniffled, and Melissa noticed a ring of white powder around the outside of his nose. "I just want to get in the club." He pulled out a small glass bottle and extended it toward Melissa. "You want a hit?"

Melissa was curious, but it was all happening so fast. Besides, Tommy was acting very strange. His eyes were like saucers, and the way he was looking at her was kind of scary. This was her first night out. She had bought a new outfit for it, and she wanted to look good, not freaky. "No, thanks," she said, as politely as she could.

"Whatever," said Tommy. Then they went into the club.

After they had paid to get in and had been checked by the security guard, the four walked through the hallway that led to the dance floor. A man wearing a brightly colored backpack walked very close to

Melissa and said, "X, coke, Special K . . ."

Melissa was startled. "No thanks," she stammered, and the man kept walking.

Melissa knew that "X" stood for Ecstasy, a hallucinogen she had read about that was supposed to put you in a good mood. And coke was cocaine, but what on earth was Special K? She knew of it only as a breakfast cereal. Suddenly Melissa felt very un-hip. But she did feel okay about asking Tonisha what it was.

"It's a drug that totally screws up your brain," Tonisha said. "Tommy did it once here, and he spent the entire night lying in a corner. He thought he was dying."

Melissa noticed that Al had caught up with the man with the backpack and was now slipping him some money. "What's he buying?" asked Melissa.

"Oh, Al really likes Ecstasy. He'll be obnoxiously nice tonight, then a total jerk all week," said Tonisha. Melissa had noticed that Al was usually in a bad mood. She had thought maybe he didn't like her.

"What does Ecstasy do?" Melissa asked.

Tonisha started to explain. "It takes you up really high and then drops you really low . . ." Then she stopped. She gave Melissa a concerned look. "Listen, I don't want to tell you what to do or anything, but I think you

34 should just stick with me and dance tonight," she said quietly. "I really like you, and I don't want you to end up as a total mess."

Melissa looked around and said, "Actually, I was just thinking the same thing. Come on, I love this song!"

So Tonisha and Melissa danced all night to deep house grooves while Tommy and Al sat on a couch, unable even to stand up. Melissa loved the spectacular light show, and the bass vibrated the floor in a way that made her feel as if her whole body was a part of the music. It kept her moving for hours.

When Melissa finally went back to the couch, Al threw his arms around her. "Melissa, I love you!" he shouted.

"Uh, yeah," said Melissa, squirming out of his embrace. They barely knew each other. His affection seemed fake and was kind of annoying. "Where's Tommy?" she asked.

"He's in the bathroom throwing up," said Al. "There was too much heroin in his coke."

Melissa began to feel very uncomfortable. "Tonisha, I think it's time to get going," she said.

"You read my mind," said Tonisha, rolling her eyes. After gathering Tommy and Al, they made their way out to the car.

Tommy threw himself into the back seat; then his nose began to bleed. "I feel really,

You can have fun—probably a lot more fun—without using drugs.

really awful . . . it's so awful," he mumbled, trying to wipe the blood from his nose on the back of his hand.

"Oh, great, what if he's OD'd," said Al in a panicked tone. "I'm Ex-ing way too hard to deal with this."

Tonisha was getting scared. "Al, will you please shut up? I'm going to the hospital," she said.

Tommy begged her not to, because his parents would kill him. Melissa said, "I'd rather see you get in trouble with your parents than watch you get really hurt."

Tommy had to spend the night in the hospital. In the car on the way home, Melissa replayed this very strange night over and over again in her mind. She knew that people who

36 | *took drugs did not always end up in the hospital. But she made a definite decision that she was not going to use any drugs from now on. It just seemed way too weird and scary.*

Besides, Melissa had had a fabulous time without using any drugs to alter her state of mind. She was amazed at how good she felt without so much as a drink or a joint. The music, the lights, and the energy of the people around her had taken her into another world. Best of all, she wouldn't have a headache later on.

Melissa wondered what was going to happen to Tommy. Would he keep doing drugs, even after almost dying tonight? Tonisha said that he would probably swear off cocaine and start doing some other drug. "Tommy is an addict, but for some reason he hasn't figured it out yet," she explained. "I don't know how scared he'll have to get to finally see what's happened to him."

CHAPTER 4

Advantages of Staying Drug-Free

The next day, Tommy called Tonisha. He didn't sound very good. Tonisha had always had a hard time figuring out how to handle the drug situation with Tommy. She did not want to lecture, but she knew he needed help. It was hard to stand back and watch him hurt himself.

"Tonisha, why don't you do drugs?" asked Tommy.

"Well, for lots of reasons," she responded carefully. She went on to describe all of her dreams and goals, and how she felt that drugs could get in the way. She also talked about how being drug-free enabled her to think more clearly, save money, and feel better all around. "For me, it just wouldn't make sense to get involved with drugs,"

38 | *Tonisha said.*

Tommy seemed to understand this. Tonisha thought that she might have helped him to understand his own situation without making him angry or defensive. She learned how powerful it can be to look at a negative situation in a positive way.

Tonisha pointed out some of the ways in which being drug-free can improve the quality of your life. Here are some more:

- *You will feel better, physically and emotionally.*

Drugs may make you feel good for a very short time, but there is always a come down that feels a hundred times worse. This is something that any former drug user will tell you.

Carrie Fisher, the actress who played Princes Leia in *Star Wars*, wrote a novel about recovering from drug addition. In the book, entitled *Postcards from the Edge*, the main character describes her painful crash:

"I was into pain reduction and mind expansion, but what I've ended up with is pain expansion and mind reduction. Everything hurts now, and nothing makes sense."

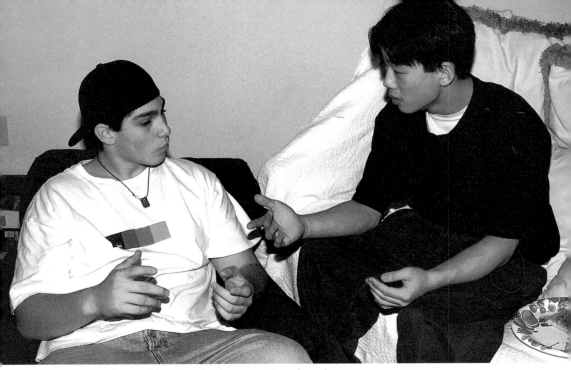

Listening to friends talk about staying drug-free may cause you to decide to stay drug-free, too.

• *You will have more money.*

Drugs are a huge drain on your finances. Many drug addicts have to steal, sometimes from people they love, to pay for their drug habits. And even if you have enough of your own money to pay for drugs, just think of what else you could do with that money.

• *You can cope better with stress.*

Life is full of little surprises, some good and some not so good. When things start to go wrong, you need all the coping skills you have to survive. Even positive changes can create stress. When you take drugs, it becomes harder to deal with all of the stress that is a natural part of life.

40 Some people use drugs to try to escape from stress. But when they come down from their high, the stress is still there. They haven't coped with the stress; they've just tried to avoid it.

• *You will have better relationships.*
A drug habit is bound to put a strain on all of your personal relationships. Often, feelings of paranoia and depression are created when you take drugs. These feelings can cause you to push away the people you really care about and the people who really care about you.

• *You can enjoy true freedom.*
Freedom is very important. You work hard so that someday you can do what *you* want to do rather than what other people have planned for you. You want to be able to choose for yourself.

But drug addiction is the opposite of freedom. An addict is letting a drug tell him or her what to do. His or her life is being controlled. Most people would rather control their own lives.

• *You can lessen the risk of contracting AIDS and other diseases.*
Even if you aren't injecting a drug into

Many people turn to drugs in order to avoid stress in their lives.

your body and sharing needles, which is an easy way to contract the HIV virus, there are other ways that taking drugs can put you at risk for AIDS and other Sexually Transmitted Diseases (STDs). If someone who is high decides to have sex, chances are he or she is not going to be very careful. It is difficult to follow safer sex precautions or even to choose abstinence if your brain is not functioning properly. It takes a clear mind to act responsibly.

- *You can learn to appreciate natural highs.*

When a person becomes addicted to drugs, she or he comes to believe that a

42 chemical high is the only way to feel good. But there are many ways to feel good that do not include health risks. They also do not involve a heavy come-down, or "crash."

- *You can lessen your risk of getting in trouble with the law.*

Nobody wants to be arrested. Nobody wants to have a criminal record, which can affect you for the rest of your life. When you take illegal drugs, you take the risk of getting caught, which can result in jail time and huge fines. You don't have time to waste sitting behind bars.

- *You can decrease the risk of dangerous and unpleasant experiences, injury, and possibly death.*

Everybody wants to have good experiences and avoid bad ones. Some people take drugs because they assume that getting high will be a good experience. But you never knows how your body will react to a drug until you take it. You may be allergic to the drug and have a terrible reaction; the drug may be fatal. You may accidentally overdose. You may have been sold a drug that was cut, or mixed, with

another dangerous chemical. You may
have a "bad trip" and feel terrified.

Even if you do have a good trip, it is
hard to come down from a high. Every
intense chemical high has an even more
intense low to go along with it. This
come-down, or crash, is not a pleasant
experience.

Finding Help

If you are abusing drugs, or if someone
you know is a drug abuser, it is not too
late to get help. The most important thing
to do is to talk to an adult you trust, such
as a parent, relative, teacher, counselor, or
religious official. If you do not feel comfortable talking to anyone in person, con-
tact one of the organizations listed in the
back of this book or look in the telephone
book under "Drug Addiction" for a list of
counseling centers in your area.

If you use drugs because it is what
everyone in your group of friends does, it
may be hard to break out of the habit.
Your friends may discourage you from
getting help. But it is your decision to
make, not theirs. Your own health and
safety are more important than fitting in.
If your friends do not understand that, it
is probably time to find new friends.

Talking about your problems may help you stay away from drugs.

As it turned out, Tommy's parents made **45**
him go into a rehabilitation program for his
drug problem. He was pretty scared, and he
still had trouble admitting to himself that
he was addicted to drugs. At first he saw a
counselor three times a week. He also had to
call the rehabilitation center every night to
check in, so that they could be sure he was
safe and sober.

His counselor helped him to figure out
what he should do to stop himself when he
felt like taking drugs. It was hard for him to
give up drugs and alcohol completely. He
came very close to starting again many
times, but each time he called his counselor
instead of his dealer, and they talked about
his feelings. He always ended up deciding
that he would be better off without taking
any drugs.

Tommy also spent a lot less time with Al,
who was still taking Ecstasy almost every
weekend. It was not easy to stay away from
someone he cared about, but being around
Al made Tommy want to take drugs. So he
ended up hanging out a lot more with
Tonisha and Melissa, and they all had a
great time together, completely sober.

As time went by, Tommy's desire to take
drugs became weaker and weaker, but it
never went away completely. He did gain

46 | *enough control over it to avoid drugs and fill his life up in other ways. He still liked to go out and have fun, and he found that he had a much better time when he wasn't falling down or passing out.*

Tommy was thinking more clearly. He was getting a better idea of what he wanted his life to be about. He realized that he could have ended up dead or seriously hurt if he hadn't changed his lifestyle, and he was grateful that he had been given a second chance.

CHAPTER 5

How Do You Say No?

*T*he connection between drugs and fashion makes it extremely difficult for teens to avoid drugs. Nobody wants to seem unfashionable, and for some groups of people, taking drugs is an important part of staying hip. Teens can be very quick to reject anyone who seems like he or she is being a "goody-goody," and nobody wants to be rejected. So how do you say no without sounding like a T-shirt or a bumper sticker?

Don't Use, Don't Judge

Tonisha was accepted by her drug-using friends, even though she did not use drugs. She never felt that her friends pushed her to use drugs, and she never

Once you decide to be drug-free, it will be easier to share your views with others.

judged her friends for what they did. She |
didn't make them feel bad about it. But
she also didn't celebrate or encourage
their drug use. She was strong, and
willing to help when Tommy was in
trouble. Tonisha is an example of somebody with her own mind and her own
style.

Choosing Your Own Style

Being *fashionable* is something you can
show on the outside, but *style* has more to
do with what you are like on the inside. It
is about your personality and attitude—
not your wardrobe.

With the right attitude and state of
mind, you can carry anything off, including being a drug-free teen in a drug-
saturated culture. When you tell people
that you don't use drugs, don't apologize
for it. Say it in a straightforward, no-
nonsense tone of voice, but do not sound
angry, condemning, or defensive.

Also, it is good to have a reason pre-
pared. You do not owe anyone an expla-
nation, but offering one can help to bring
about a kind of understanding between
you and a new friend or acquaintance.
For example, saying, "I really don't like
what acid does to my mind," or "I can't

50 afford to spend $30 for a hit of Ecstasy," will tell someone else a great deal about who you are and how you think. It might also prevent people who use drugs from thinking that you look down on them. In fact, it might even cause them to reconsider their own reasons for taking drugs.

Once you make up your mind to be a drug-free person, it will become easier to share that part of yourself with other people. If you believe in yourself and in your decisions, people will usually respect you for it, even if they don't tell you so. Not taking drugs is part of who you are, and there is no reason to feel guilty or ashamed. And if somebody does reject you because you do not take drugs, you might want to think about whether you really want to know or trust that person.

Pressure from Peers

Many people who have a group of friends who use drugs have a hard time giving up drugs because it means that they have to leave the group. They cannot remain friends with the same people, because there would be too much temptation to start taking drugs again. This is one reason that many people stay addicted to drugs or alcohol for their entire lives.

Even if they want to stop, they are not ready to change their lives totally and leave their old friends and activities behind.

One way to avoid this situation is by not taking up drugs to begin with. If you have already started, it is never too late to quit, no matter how deeply you are into it. Many people are willing to help you break a drug or an alcohol habit. Talk with a school counselor, teacher, minister, rabbi, priest, or parent. They will be able to tell you where to seek help. Or see the "Where to Go for Help" section at the back of this book.

There are plenty of fashionable people out there who do not take drugs. Sometimes it's easier to make new friends than to cope with a dangerous habit. You need to consider your own health and safety first. The drug of the moment probably is not worth a lifetime of pain.

CHAPTER 6

Alternatives to Drug Highs

It is true that everybody needs to feel "up" in some way. But you don't have to use drugs to feel this way. There are other ways of having fun, feeling pleasure, and experiencing new feelings. And those ways *can* be completely safe when done properly.

Physical Activity
When you engage in physical activity of any kind, your body releases endorphins, chemicals that make you feel energetic and powerful. This type of natural high can result from many activities, from sports to dancing.

Sports and Fitness
Joggers often rave about the buzz they get from running. This is something that

When you exercise, your body releases endorphins, chemicals that make you feel energetic and powerful.

weight lifters and athletes of all kinds also enjoy, sometimes every day. Talk to your gym teacher or doctor about a physical fitness program, or find a sport you like and work at it. Just about any sport should be able to get that feeling flowing, besides helping you meet others who enjoy the same sport that you do.

Drug-free Dancing

Dancing is another activity that helps your body to release endorphins, and you don't need professional lessons to do it. Just create your own style of moving to music. If you can find an all-ages night-club where you can dance, there will probably be flashing lights and an excit-

54 ing atmosphere to enhance the experience. Otherwise, your favorite CD and a few good friends can be all the nightclub you need. Wherever you are, just letting yourself move to great music can make you feel energetic, happy, powerful, excited, and sometimes weightless. These are sensations often described by drug users, but they can be enjoyed without drugs when you really get into dancing.

There is a certain glamour and thrill in getting dressed up and going out. Many big-city nightclubbers claim to be more addicted to clothes and makeup than they are to drugs. If you don't have nightclubs to go to, wear something fun to a concert. Or really make an entrance at your school dance. All it takes is a little imagination— fashion and style can give you a drug-free high.

Arts and Entertainment

Many people take drugs to be entertained. But our society surrounds us with arts and entertainment, so there are plenty of options that do not pose the kind of risks that drugs do.

One of the most popular forms of entertainment in our society today is television. While many people still debate whether the effects of television are negative or positive, most agree that, in moderation, watching television can be a harmless and enjoyable pastime.

Many young people have taken to "channel surfing," which means flipping through channels very quickly with a remote control. In a way, doing this allows you to watch television as it was not intended to be watched, and to create your own shows from the pieces.

Movies are another drug-free way to escape reality for a few hours. You can be completely transported into another place, time, or dimension. Of course, reading a book is a more exciting way to achieve that state, because you use your imagination to create the sights and sounds. The human imagination is much more vivid than any recording device. The right book at the right time can change the way you perceive reality.

All types of art can have this mind-expanding effect. Walking through an art museum can be like taking a psychedelic trip, involving wild emotional swings and distortions of time and space. Art can take you all over the world and through a wide range of thoughts and feelings.

Creating art can also give you a non-

56 | chemical rush. You might enjoy taking a painting class or learning to play a musical instrument. Creating something can give you a way to express yourself, and the possibilities for creative expression are limitless.

Social Highs

Human beings have a strong need to interact and communicate with one another, and this is one reason that many young people turn to drugs. They may drink at a party hoping to loosen up and break the tension, share a joint because they think it will make their conversation "deeper," or take Ecstasy and hug complete strangers.

But no drugs can really help us to communicate. They only make it more confusing and difficult. Besides, people have been connecting for centuries without using drugs. The next time you go to a social event, try to observe the people who are drinking or using other drugs. How are they acting? What kind of impression are they making on the people around them?

Meeting new people or spending time with friends can be a high in itself, and it is a high best experienced without drugs or alcohol. Seeing the world through someone else's eyes is true mind-expansion, and taking drugs can only make getting to know people more difficult in the end. Nobody's true personality can emerge when they are drunk or stoned.

Cyberspace

"Surfing the Net" is a term coined to describe scanning the Internet for information of all kinds and sometimes communicating with other Internet users. This is cutting-edge entertainment, and it can be thrilling to discover other worlds and communicate with new people this way.

All of these ideas are just a starting point. There are endless possibilities in life for having fun without drugs. The ultimate high comes from creating your own style and shaping your life into the way you want it to be.

Glossary—
Explaining New Words

convulsions   A series of uncontrollable muscle contractions.

culture   The beliefs, customs, and characteristics of a social group.

depression   A mental illness marked by feelings of sadness, difficulty sleeping, and other conditions.

identity   The distinct personality of a person.

mainstream   The dominant or most common behaviors and attitudes in a society.

moderation   Avoiding extremes in behavior or beliefs.

paranoia   A feeling of irrational suspiciousness.

pastime   An activity that provides interest or amusement.

psychedelic Something that produces abnormal mental states involving distorted sights or sounds.

rebelliousness Opposition to authority; defiance.

rehabilitation The process of being restored to health after a period of addiction to a harmful drug or after a serious illness.

style A distinctive manner of expression, behavior, or fashion.

subculture A social group that practices behaviors that are different from the behaviors of mainstream society.

Where to Go for Help

If you need help right away, call one of these hot lines, or look in the white pages of the phone book under "Drug Abuse" or "Community Service Numbers."
(800) ALCOHOL
(800) COCAINE
(800) 448-4663 (Youth Crisis Hot Line)

Alcoholics Anonymous
Box 459, Grand Central Station
New York, NY 10163
(212) 870-3400
e-mail: 76245-2153@compuserve.com
Web site: http://www.alcoholics-
    anonymous.org

Narcotics Anonymous
19737 Nordhoff Place
Chatsworth, CA 91311
(818) 773-9999
e-mail: wso@aol.com

National Clearinghouse for Alcohol and
    Drug Information
P.O. Box 2345
Rockville, MD 20847-2345
(301) 468-2600
e-mail: info@prevline.health.org
Web site: http://www/health.org

National Council on Alcoholism and
    Drug Dependence
12 West 21st Street
New York, NY 10010
(800) 622-2255
e-mail: national@NCADD.org
Web site: http://www.hcadd.org

In Canada:
Alcohol and Drug Dependency Informa-
    tion and Counseling Services
    (ADDICS)
2471 1/2 Portage Avenue, #2
Winnipeg, Manitoba R3J ON 6
(204) 942-4730

Narcotics Anonymous
P.O. Box 7500
Station A
Toronto, ON M5W 1P9
(416) 691-9519

For Further Reading

Benson, Kathleen, and James Haskins. *The Sixties Reader*. New York: Viking Kestrel, 1988.

Cheney, Glenn Alan. *Drugs, Teens, and Recovery: Real-Life Stories of Trying to Stay Clean*. Hillside, N.J.: Enslow Publishers, 1993.

Cohen, Susan, *What You Can Believe About Drugs: An Honest and Unhysterical Guide for Teens*. New York: M. Evans, 1987.

Frisch, Carlienne. *Drugs and Music*. New York: Rosen Publishing Group, 1995.

Myers, Arthur. *Drugs and Peer Pressure*. New York: Rosen Publishing Group, 1995.

Polhemus, Ted. *Street Style*. New York: Thames and Hudson Inc., 1994.

Index

About the Author
George Glass is a freelance writer living in New York City.

Photo Credits
Cover by Seth Dinnerman; p. 16 by Archive Photos; p. 30 by Olga M. Vega; pp. 35, 39 by Ira Fox; all other photos by Seth Dinnerman.